How Many
GUINEA PIGS
Can Fit
ON A PLANE?

ANSWERS TO YOUR MOST
CLEVER MATH QUESTIONS

LAURA OVERDECK

Feiwel and Friends

NEW YORK

A Feiwel and Friends Book
An imprint of Macmillan Publishing Group, LLC

Printed in the United States of America by LSC Communications,
Crawfordsville, Indiana. For information, address Feiwel and Friends,
175 Fifth Avenue, New York, N.Y. 10010.

Our books may be purchased in bulk for promotional, educational,
or business use. Please contact your local bookseller or the Macmillan
Corporate and Premium Sales Department at (800) 221-7945 ext. 5442
or by e-mail at MacmillanSpecialMarkets@macmillan.com.

Library of Congress Cataloging-in-Publication Data

Names: Overdeck, Laura.
Title: How many guinea pigs can fit on a plane? : answers to your most
clever math questions / Laura Overdeck.
Description: New York : Feiwel and Friends, [2017] |
Audience: Age 7-11. | Includes bibliographical references.
Identifiers: LCCN 2016035835 |
ISBN 978-1-250-07229-0 (hardcover) | ISBN 978-1-250-12368-8 (pbk.)
Subjects: LCSH: Mathematics—Miscellanea—Juvenile literature.
Classification: LCC QA99 .O94 2017 | DDC 513—dc23
LC record available at https://lccn.loc.gov/2016035835

Book design by Raphael Geroni

Photographs from shutterstock.com, istockphoto.com, and
Laura Overdeck

Feiwel and Friends logo designed by Filomena Tuosto

First Edition—2017

1 3 5 7 9 10 8 6 4 2

mackids.com

Thank you to all our Bedtime Math fans,
especially those who asked the wild,
imaginative questions in this book.
I couldn't have written it without you!

Contents

Introduction

IF YOU'VE EVER WONDERED ABOUT some crazy things—like how many bees it would take to fill a jar with honey, or how long it would take to fly to Pluto—this book is for you.

But did you know that you can figure out the answers to these and all kinds of other questions yourself?

It's all about math, and it's all about fun.

The questions in this book all came from fans of Bedtime Math (bedtimemath.org). Real kids wrote to us, and we've gathered some of their questions here. Since the numbers get big fast, we walk you through the math so you can learn how to solve these wacky questions on your own—and discover some cool facts along the way!

Check out the crazy questions and very surprising answers in this book. Soon you'll know how to figure out just about any question, because math is power.

Have fun with the numbers!

A Bite of Pi

ONE COOL NUMBER YOU'LL SEE IN THIS book is *pi*. If you take the width of a circle, pi is the number of circle widths you would need to tie end to end to wrap around the circle exactly once. It's 3.14159265. . . . The digits go on forever, but we can just use 3.14.

Pi does much more than help you find the distance around a circle. It helps measure round objects in all kinds of ways.

The widest distance across a circle or sphere (ball) is its diameter. The distance halfway across a circle or sphere is its radius. Both pi and the radius are super important, as you'll see here!

The distance around a circle (the circumference) is exactly that magic number, pi, times its width (diameter):

pi × diameter.

The area of a circle is

pi × the radius × the radius again.

The surface area of a sphere (the amount of wrapping paper you'd need to cover it perfectly) is

4 × pi × radius × radius again.

Finally, the volume of a sphere (space taken up by a ball) is

⅘ × pi × radius × radius again × radius again.

Now we can use these cool facts to answer some crazy questions!

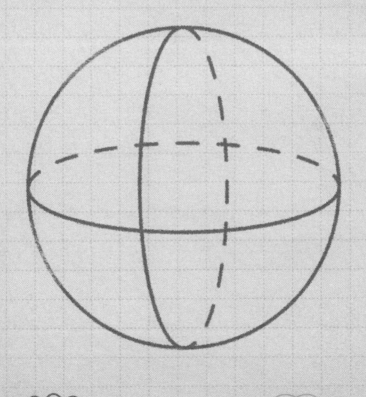

CHAPTER 1

....

ANIMAL MATH

"How many guinea pigs can fit on a plane?"

—Andrew L.

IF EACH GUINEA PIG SITS IN ITS OWN SEAT, THEN IT just depends on the number of seats on the plane. But what if these furry fellows squish in as tightly as possible? Guinea pigs are happiest when they're together with friends. In fact, in Switzerland it's illegal to own only 1 guinea pig because this is considered cruel. So let's pack those pigs into the plane.

If each fur ball is 8 inches long, 4 inches wide, and 4 inches tall, and each one lies right up against the next, then in a 1-foot cube of space we can fit 3 pigs across, 3 pigs top to bottom, and 1½ pigs front to back. That comes to

3 × 3 × 1½ = 13½ guinea pigs per cubic foot.

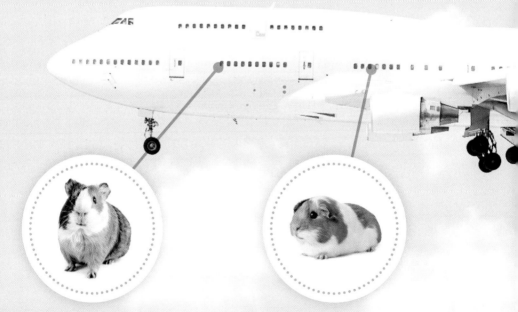

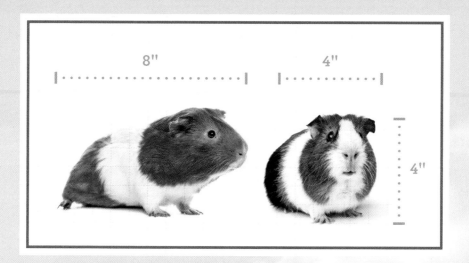

8"

4"

4"

A 747 jet has about 1,000 cubic meters of space total for passengers and suitcases, or about 35,000 cubic feet. That gives us

A: 35,000 × 13½ guinea pigs in each = **472,500 GUINEA PIGS.**

No guinea pig will feel lonely on that airplane. Let's just make sure somebody is flying it.

"How many birds would it take to pick you up and fly with you?"

—Kaien M.

THAT DEPENDS ON 2 THINGS: HOW MUCH YOU weigh and how much each bird can carry. Birds come in all sizes, and some have stronger wings than others. A tiny hummingbird struggles to fly after nibbling a few berries; let's say it can carry about 1 ounce (the weight of 2 tablespoons of water). On the other hand, the female harpy eagle weighs 20 pounds and can carry small animals that weigh nearly as much; let's say it can fly with 10 pounds. So if you weigh 60 pounds . . .

1 pound has 16 ounces, so 60 × 16 = 960 ounces.

A: It will take 960 hummingbirds to lift you.

But each harpy eagle can pick up 10 pounds of your weight.

A: 60 pounds ÷ 10 pounds per eagle = **6 EAGLES**

You'll need only 6 eagles to pick you up—and those eagles might carry you higher, too.

Q: "How many bees does it take to make one jar of honey?"

—Nina J.

WHEN PEOPLE WORK REALLY HARD, WE SAY they're "busy as a bee"—but the bee is probably the busier one. These cute, stripey friends of ours spread pollen from one flower to the next, helping fruits and veggies grow as they collect nectar and pollen to feed their family and friends. Honeybees turn the sugary nectar into honey by passing it from one bee's mouth to another's, then drying it out by fanning their wings 118 times per second. That said, in its short 6-week life of hard work, a bee makes only 1/12 teaspoon of honey! So . . .

12 bees make 1 teaspoon.

A tablespoon has 3 teaspoons, so

12 × 3 = 36 bees make 1 tablespoon.

A jar of honey weighing 8 ounces has about 10 tablespoons, so

A: 36 bees × 10 tablespoons = **360 BEES** make 1 jar.

Luckily, a hive has so many bees—up to 60,000 by summer—that one hive can make enough honey for itself and plenty of extra for us!

Q: "How many twigs are in a bird's nest?"

—Sophie O.

FIRST, LET'S DECIDE WHICH KIND OF NEST WE NEED here. There are scrape nests, where birds dig a hole in the dirt; mound nests, where they push together a pile of dirt—okay, those types have zero sticks. Sophie's asking about platform and cupped nests, the bowl-shaped nests made of sticks and other material. An eagle's nest runs around 5 feet wide and 4 feet deep, which is huge. But your everyday robin's nest is just 6 to 8 inches wide.

A: One website says a robin needs to gather about **350 TWIGS OR BLADES OF DRIED GRASS,** then glues all those pieces together with mud.

If that sounds like a lot of work, imagine how the eagle feels.

How far does a bird fly to build a 350-stick nest?

If a bird has to fly 50 feet to reach each perfectly sized twig, and then 50 feet back to the nest, the bird flies 100 feet on every trip.

For 350 sticks, that gives us

350 × 100 = 35,000 feet.

A mile has 5,280 feet, so let's see how many mile-long chunks the bird flew:

35,000 ÷ 5,280 = ABOUT 6½ MILES.

The bird flies more than 6 miles to build that nest, not counting the trips to get mud—and if it rains hard, they need to fetch mud all over again!

"How many spiders are there in the whole world?"

—Charlie Y.

SPIDERS AREN'T THE PRETTIEST ANIMALS. BUT most spiders are our friends, since they eat bugs that we don't like. So maybe it's okay that no matter where you are, people say there's a spider within 3 feet of you. Spider-counting scientists have tried to figure out whether that's true. They found an average of 1 wolf spider for every 2 square meters of ice in the Arctic, and 3 for each square meter in Europe (a meter is a little more than 3 feet). Earth has more than 40,000 different types, or species, of spiders. Another scientist averaged out the numbers for all the different species and came up with about 130 spiders per square meter, so . . .

A kilometer is 1,000 meters. So a square kilometer has

1,000 × 1,000 = 1,000,000 square meters (1 million).

So each square kilometer has 130,000,000 spiders (130 million).

149,000,000
square
kilometers

Earth has 149,000,000 of those square kilometers on land, so

A: 149,000,000 × 130,000,000 = **ABOUT 19,000,000,000,000,000 SPIDERS.**

That's 19 *quadrillion*. If you think that's a huge number, try counting up their legs!

Q: "How many dogs are there in the whole world?"

—Kaiya and Keiry R.

ALTHOUGH THE UNITED STATES OFFICIALLY counts up many types of its pets, not all other countries do. Some researchers have tried to guess, coming up with

525 million pet dogs!

This includes

110 MILLION in China

78 MILLION in the United States

32 MILLION in India

30 MILLION in Brazil

12 MILLION in Russia

9½ MILLION in Japan

9 MILLION in South Africa

9 MILLION in France

7 MILLION in the United Kingdom

And that's not counting the millions of stray dogs.

If there are 525 million dogs in the whole world and if the dog owners have only 1 dog each, how many puppies would have to be born for every person in the world to have a dog?

• •

The world has about 8 billion people, or 8,000,000,000, so how many more people than dogs are there?

8,000,000,000 – 525,000,000 = 7,475,000,000 people without dogs

So we need

7,475,000,000 new puppies for everyone to have a dog.

If ½ the 525,000,000 dogs are female and can have puppies, how many puppies would each female need to have?

We take ½ the total to find the number of females:

525,000,000 dogs × ½ = 262,500,000 female dogs

So how many puppies would each of the 262,500,000 mama dogs have to have to add up to 7,475,000,000?

7,475,000,000 ÷ 262,500,000 mama dogs = about 28½ puppies per mama dog

So every mama dog would have to have 29 puppies for everyone to have a dog!

Q: "If a ladybug were me-sized, how many dots would it have?"

—Lucy P.

LADYBUGS LIKE TO BE A BIT TRICKY: SOME HAVE NO dots at all, and some have as many as 26! And those dots have to fit on a very small area—a ladybug's 2 wings cover a circle about a quarter inch wide, which works out to be about 1/20 of a 1-inch-by-1-inch square. We humans have a lot more skin, or *surface area*, than that—and we can use math to find out how much we have. You take a certain fraction of your height and weight, and multiply that by other numbers. It's a very grown-up equation, but it tells us that the average 9-year-old kid has about 1,200 square inches of skin. So . . .

1/20 of a 1-inch-
by-1-inch square

However many dots ⅟₂₀ of a square inch has, a full square inch has 20 times as many.

If the ladybug has 10 dots, a full square inch would have

10 dots × 20 = 200 dots.

A: Then 1,200 square inches of skin would have 1,200 × 200 = **240,000 DOTS.**

I F YOU'VE EVER LOOKED IN THE MIRROR AT YOUR teeth, then looked inside a dog's mouth, or a hamster's, or (gulp) an alligator's mouth, you know that we all have different numbers of teeth. You have 20 teeth as a kid, and once you lose your baby teeth, you'll have between 28 and 32 grown-up teeth.

A: A Komodo dragon, which is a big, dangerous lizard, has **ALMOST 60 TEETH.**

Tooth-Paste

But some animals have even more. A shark has between 15 and 50 "front" teeth (most have around 20 or 30), but each tooth can have 5 or more teeth behind it!

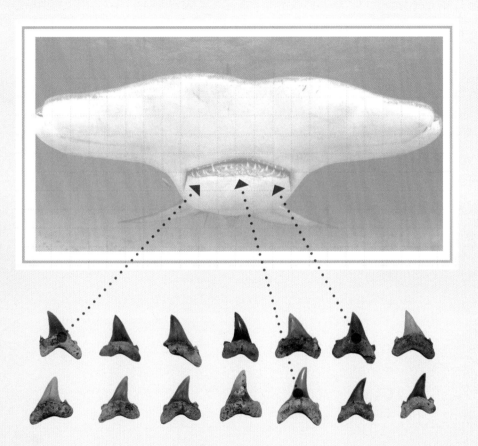

So how many teeth can a shark have?

If there are 30 teeth in front,

30 + (30 × 5) = 180 TEETH.

Even crazier, a shark loses those teeth over and over. It might grow 200 new sets in its life. So that would come to

180 × 200 = 36,000 teeth!

"How long does it take a deer to grow antlers?"

—Emerson B.

ANTLERS GROW FASTER THAN ANY OTHER MAMMAL bone—up to 1 inch per day. On a moose, that adds up to a whole *pound* a day, growing to as much as 80 pounds! Deer antlers weigh between only 3 and 9 pounds, and usually only male deer ("bucks") grow them. In the spring, the deer's brain senses that there's more daylight and signals the body to start growing antlers; that's when antlers grow fastest. Deer shed the antlers anytime between December and March.

A: **Deer antlers grow for 4 to 5 months, roughly from March to the end of August.**

If antlers grow 1 inch per day, how many feet and inches would they be after a month?

30 days × 1 inch per day = 30 inches per month

Every 12 inches is 1 foot, so

30 inches = 12 + 12 + 6 = 2 FEET 6 INCHES.

That's about as tall as you were at 1 year old!

"If I were as strong as an ant, how much could I pick up?"

—Sophia Y.

ANTS CAN'T PICK UP MUCH MORE THAN a crumb, a tiny leaf, or a piece of a twig. But ants are tiny, so lifting those things is a big deal. Some ants can carry up to 50 or even 100 times their own weight! What would that look like for you? Take your weight in pounds and multiply it by 50:

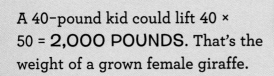

A 40-pound kid could lift 40 × 50 = **2,000 POUNDS**. That's the weight of a grown female giraffe.

A 60-pound kid could lift **3,000 POUNDS**—the weight of a 4-door compact car.

A 100-pound kid could lift **5,000 POUNDS**—the weight of an adult male Indian rhinoceros.

A 200-pound adult could lift **10,000 POUNDS**—the weight of a grown-up male Asian elephant.

IT DEPENDS ON HOW DIRTY AND SMELLY THAT DOG can get, and how much the dog *likes* being dirty and smelly . . . and how much the owner doesn't mind. Dog experts say dogs shouldn't take too many baths, because the soap washes off too much oil from their fur. But they do need at least 1 bath every 3 months. How many baths is that in a year?

A year has 12 months.

So there are 12 ÷ 3 = 4 sets of 3 months, giving us **4 BATHS PER YEAR.**

The next question is, how many baths do *you* take? Anything you do once a day, you do 365 times in a year . . . or about 1,000 times every 3 years. So whether it's sneezing, taking a bath, or eating ice cream, it adds up fast!

"What moves faster, a hopping bunny or a running person?"

—Inaya K.

IF YOUR PET BUNNY IS ON THE LOOSE, YOU'D better know the answer to this question. Most bunnies, such as the cottontail rabbit, run around 18 to 20 miles an hour—about the speed of cars on streets with houses. But their cousins, the hares, run much faster: A jackrabbit can zoom at almost 40 miles an hour!

Now how about people? Usain Bolt, the record-breaking Olympian, ran the 100-meter dash (328 feet) in 9.58 seconds. How many miles an hour is that? Here's a handy fact: 22 feet per second is exactly 15 miles an hour. So 44 feet per second is double that (30 miles an hour), 66 feet per second is triple (45 miles an hour), and so on. Where does Usain line up with that?

Usain ran 328 feet, and if we round his time up to 10 seconds, he ran almost exactly 33 feet per second— which is 1½ as much as 22 feet per second.

328 feet ÷ 10 seconds = 32.8 or 33 feet per second

1½ × 15 miles an hour = 22½ miles an hour

A: So Usain Bolt, the fastest person ever, is only a little faster than the slowest rabbits.

And hares are *much* faster than we are!

Q: "If all the elephants in the world were standing in a line, how long would the line of elephants be?"

—Finley M.

ALTHOUGH OUR WORLD USED TO HAVE UP to 5 million elephants, sadly their population is now threatened. There are only about 470,000 African elephants today, and about 40,000 Asian elephants. If you lined up those elephants, though, that beautiful line would stretch a long way.

Elephants range from 16 to 24 feet long. We can count the length as 20 feet, but if we add another 5 feet for the trunk holding the next elephant's tail, then each elephant spans 25 feet. Rounding to 500,000 elephants, we can find the length of that whole line:

25 feet × 500,000 = 12,500,000 feet (12½ million feet).

25 feet

A mile has 5,280 feet, so we can divide by 5,280 feet to find how many mile-long chunks we have:

A: 12,500,000 ÷ 5,280 = **2,367 MILES.**
That's almost the length of the United States!

CHAPTER 2

NATURE GONE WILD

Q: "How fast does the fastest tree in the world grow?"

—Mihira and Siona T.

A: The empress tree can grow almost 20 feet in its first year, and anywhere from 2 to 7 feet each year after that. It can have crazy growth spurts of 11 to 12 inches in just 3 weeks!

Imagine if that happened to you!

Just to compare, when people think something is slow and boring, they say "it's like watching grass grow."

Grass can grow up to 3½ inches in a week. How much is that in 3 weeks?

3½ inches × 3 = 10½ INCHES IN 3 WEEKS, **about the same as a speedy empress tree!**

But if you think about it, that comes to

3½ inches in a week ÷ 7 days per week ÷ 24 hours per day = 0.02 inches in an hour.

That's ⅟₅₀ of an inch an hour, which would be hard to see either in the grass or on the tree!

Q:
"How many states in the U.S. have snow?"
—Carrie S.

A: It turns out that every U.S. state has had snow at some time in history!

That's because most states have at least one mountain, where at the peak the air gets cold. Of course, the really warm states get very little snow. All the southernmost states have nearly zero annual snowfall: Florida, Alabama, Mississippi, Louisiana, Texas, New Mexico, Arizona, and way out in the ocean, Hawaii. Most areas in Alabama, for instance, get a fraction of an inch at most. By comparison, 6 other states have had 4 feet of snow or more fall in 1 day: Alaska, California, Colorado, New Hampshire, Montana, and Washington.

Washington's Mount Rainier wins with the most snow per year: It gets 671 inches on average. How tall is that in feet?

There are 12 inches in a foot, so we want to know how many 12-inch chunks fit into 671 inches. Let's start with a straight 600 inches:

600 inches ÷ 12 inches per foot = 50 feet

Just as 600 is divisible by 12, so is 60 feet:

60 inches ÷ 12 inches per foot = 5 feet

So 55 feet gets us to 660 inches. We still have another 11 inches to get to 671, which adds almost 1 more foot.

So Mount Rainier gets about

50 + 5 + 1 = 56 FEET OF SNOW A YEAR.

That's about 2 to 3 times the height of a 2-story house!

"How many raindrops does it take to fill a glass of water?"

—Jay A.

THERE ISN'T ONE EXACT SIZE OF RAINDROP, but we can make a guess. If a raindrop is a tiny ball 2 millimeters (mm) across (less than ⅒ inch), its radius is 1 mm. Then its volume is

⁴⁄₃ × pi (that's 3.14) × 1 mm × 1 mm × 1 mm.

(See volume of a sphere in "A Bite of Pi," p. 2.)

That comes to about 4 little millimeter-sized cubes of water.

A milli*liter* (ml) is the same as 1 cubic centimeter, which holds 10 mm by 10 mm by 10 mm = 1,000 cubic millimeters. So how many raindrops fill a milliliter?

1,000 cubic mm ÷ 4 cubic mm per raindrop = about 250 raindrops fill 1 milliliter.

A milliliter is tiny. There are 240 milliliters in an 8-ounce cup. So you need . . .

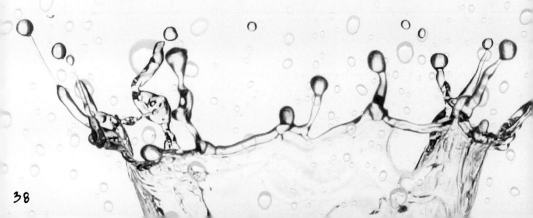

250 raindrops in every ml × 240 ml in a glass= **60,000 RAINDROPS** to fill an 8-ounce glass.

It might be easier to drink from the faucet.

"How many spider webs does it take to weigh the same amount as a banana?"

—Everett V.

SPIDER WEBS ARE AMONG THE STRONGEST materials in nature—and yet a cubic inch of spider silk weighs about ⅔ of an ounce; just to compare, that's about ⅙ as much as a cubic inch of steel. So how many cubic inches would you need to match the weight of a banana? Bananas weigh about 4 ounces, including the peel. So we just divide to find out how many ⅔-ounce chunks to pack together:

4 ÷ ⅔ = 6

A: We need just **6 CUBIC INCHES OF SPIDER WEB.**

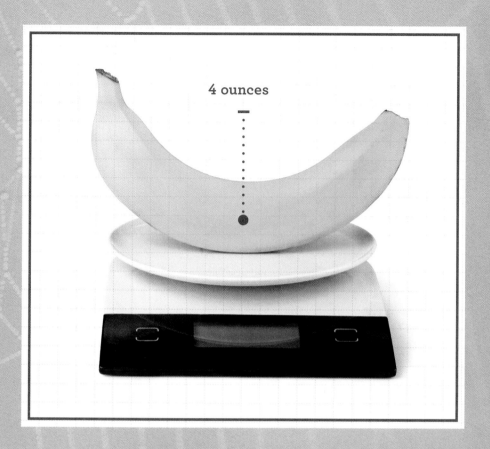

4 ounces

By the way, those 4 ounces of silk could stretch 5,000 miles—that's across the United States and back!

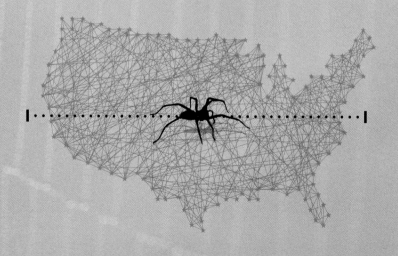

THE BIGGER THE TREE, THE MORE LEAVES IT HAS. Luckily for us, foresters have a trick to guess the number of leaves on a tree. First, we find the surface area of the tree if it were ball shaped: Multiply the radius of that ball of leaves by the radius again, then by pi, then by 4. (See "A Bite of Pi," p. 2.) Then you guess how many of that tree's leaves could cover a flat 1-foot square. Multiply that by that surface area to find how many leaves would cover that ball. After all, the tree needs just enough leaves to catch every ray of sun from every direction. So whether they're at the edge of the tree or farther in toward the trunk, if you pushed them all to the outside, they should roughly cover the whole outer shell. Let's try it with a 50-foot-wide oak tree:

The circle under the oak has a radius of 25 feet (half its diameter of 50 feet). So its area is

pi (that's 3.14) x 25 x 25 feet = 1,962½ square feet.

4 times that number would cover the ball made by the tree's branches:

1,962½ x 4 = 7,850 square feet.

Let's say it takes 10 oak leaves to cover a square foot. That size tree would have . . .

A: 7,850 square feet x 10 leaves in each square foot = **78,500 LEAVES.**

Of course, the tree won't be so perfect at leaf-growing that it will have no extras. It might have 2 or 3 times as many leaves; some say a large oak can have as many as 200,000 leaves! Different trees also have crowns of different shapes, like pointy cones and tall cylinders. But your guess will be close enough to show that you'll need help raking up those leaves when they fall!

"How far are the clouds from us?"

—Anoushka M.

CLOUDS ARE JUST BATCHES OF VERY, VERY TEENY water droplets and ice crystals floating in the air. We can have clouds right here around us on the ground—that's called fog. But if we're talking about clouds up in the sky, we have a few different types.

Nimbostratus are the rain clouds that start around **2,000 FEET UP** and make a thick gray layer.

Wispy cirrus clouds float at **18,000 FEET AND UP.**

Giant storm clouds called cumulonimbus can tower **60,000 FEET** into the sky!

How long does it take rain falling from up there to land on our umbrellas?

The biggest raindrops fall at 20 miles an hour—and they do not look like a ball or a teardrop. The air pushing up on them flattens them out like a hamburger bun!

A mile is 5,280 feet long, so first we find out how many miles the raindrop fell. If it came from a cumulonimbus, for example . . .

60,000 feet ÷ 5,280 feet per mile = a little more than 11 miles

If a raindrop can fall 20 miles in 1 hour, it will fall 11 miles in $^{11}\!/_{20}$ of an hour:

60 minutes per hour × $^{11}\!/_{20}$ hours = 33 MINUTES

So that raindrop that just splashed you could have started falling a half hour ago!

THAT DEPENDS ON THE SPEED OF THE WIND AND the size of the blades, or "rotors," on your windmill. The bigger the area the rotors sweep, the more power you get. At the same time, the faster the wind blows, the faster the blades spin, and the more power you get.

Someone figured out a cool equation to find the power in watts:

0.0052 × the area swept (in square feet) × the wind speed (in miles per hour) × wind speed again × wind speed again

rotors

That means when you double the wind speed, you get 2 × 2 × 2 = 8 times the power!

So if you have a windmill that makes a 10-foot-wide circle, the rotor area will be

pi (that's 3.14) × 5 feet × 5 feet = 78½ square feet.

And if the wind blows it at 15 miles an hour, your power will be

0.0052 × 78½ × 15 × 15 × 15 = 1,378 watts.

If you use 75-watt bulbs in your house, that will come to

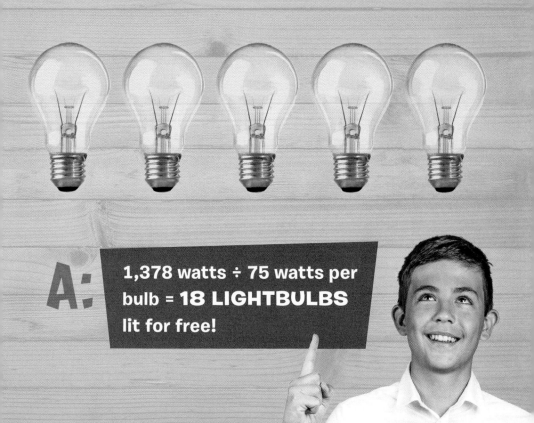

A: 1,378 watts ÷ 75 watts per bulb = **18 LIGHTBULBS** lit for free!

"Which wind blows faster, a tornado or a hurricane?"

—Carolyn L.

WIND CAN BLOW AT ALL DIFFERENT SPEEDS. The Beaufort scale gives each of them a name:

A breeze blows up to 31 miles an hour.

Once a breeze reaches about 23 miles an hour, flags blow straight to the side.

A near gale blows up to 38 miles an hour.

A severe gale reaches up to 54 miles an hour.

A violent storm blows up to 72 miles an hour.

A hurricane is any wind that blows 73 miles an hour or stronger.

The fastest hurricane winds ever measured clocked in at 253 miles per hour during Tropical Cyclone Olivia in 1996 (a cyclone is a hurricane in the South Pacific or Indian Ocean). The fastest tornado winds blew 318 miles an hour during a 1999 tornado in Oklahoma.

318 miles an hour

A: So the **TORNADO** wins by 318 - 253 = **65 MILES AN HOUR FASTER**.

"How many gallons of water does it take to put out a fire?"

—Selah and Abi H.

FIREFIGHTERS HAVE A HANDY WAY TO FIGURE THIS out: They take the area the fire covers and divide by 3. That gives them the number of gallons of water per minute that they need to spray. So if there's a fire that covers a rectangle 20 feet wide and 60 feet long:

20 × 60 = 1,200 square feet

1,200 ÷ 3 = 400 gallons per minute are needed.

It turns out that the color of the cap on a fire hydrant can tell you how fast it pumps water. For example, in one city's system:

 **Red = less than 500 gallons per minute (gpm)**

 **Green = 1,000– 1,500 gpm**

 **Yellow = 500– 999 gpm**

 **Blue = more than 1,500 gpm**

So if a whole 2-story house that's 30 feet wide and 60 feet long is on fire, which of these hydrants do you need?

30 × 60 = 1,800 square feet

1,800 × 2 floors = 3,600 square feet in total

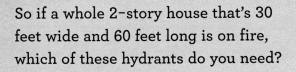

A: 3,600 ÷ 3 = **1,200 GALLONS PER MINUTE**

How long firefighters have to spray depends on the type of fire, but they'll need at least a green-capped fire hydrant.

CHAPTER 3

MATH FOR YOUR MOUTH

Q: "What would 85 pounds (my weight) of chocolate look like on the cocoa plant?"

—Ryan and Dylan T.

FIRST WE NEED TO KNOW HOW MANY COCOA BEANS make a pound of chocolate. It turns out that a 2-ounce dark-chocolate bar needs 12¼ beans to make it. When you open the cacao pods from the tree and mash down the beans, however, you lose some of the beans, such as the ones the bugs started to nibble. So you have to start with about 17 beans to make that 2-ounce bar. Now we need to figure out how many 2-ounce chocolate bars match your weight.

1 pound has 16 ounces.

16 ÷ 2 = 8 chocolate bars per pound

If you weigh 85 pounds, you weigh 85 sets of those bars, so 85 × 8 = 680 chocolate bars.

Each bar uses 17 beans, so 680 × 17 = 11,560 beans.

= 17 ×

20–60
beans

A pod can hold anywhere between 20 and 60 beans.
Let's say it holds 40 beans on average. That means

A: 11,560 beans ÷ 40 beans per pod = 289
cacao pods. A tree on average grows
about 30 pods, so it takes almost 10
trees to make your weight in chocolate!

"How much chocolate does the average person eat each day? And if I eat 15 times that, how much chocolate do I eat in a year?"

—Jillian T.

IT DEPENDS WHAT COUNTRY YOU CALL home. In America, the average person eats 9½ pounds of chocolate every year. How much is that, really?

9½ pounds × 16 ounces per pound = 152 ounces

Dividing by 365 days, we get

A: 152 ounces ÷ 365 days = **ABOUT ⅖ OF AN OUNCE** a day, or a few bites of a candy bar.

Hey, that's not so crazy. But if you eat *15 times* as much chocolate as other people, that comes to

152 ounces a year × 15 = 2,280 ounces a year.

A: 2,280 ounces ÷ 16 ounces in a pound = **142½ POUNDS** a year!

How much chocolate is that every day?

2,280 ounces ÷ 365 days per year =

about 6 ounces every day.

People in Switzerland seem to like chocolate the most. They eat nearly 20 pounds of chocolate per year—more than double what the average American eats!

Q: "About how much food do we eat every day?"

—Vasily M.

EVERY ANIMAL OUT THERE, INCLUDING you, eats some amount of food every year.

A: The average American eats almost 2,000 pounds of food in a year, which comes to more than **5 POUNDS A DAY**.

Just to compare, elephants eat between 165 and 330 pounds of food a day!

How much does an elephant eat in a year?

If we go with 250 pounds on average,

250 pounds × 365 days = MORE THAN 91,000 POUNDS PER YEAR.

To compare with other big animals, hippos eat 88 pounds of food a day, while giraffes eat 75 pounds.

"What's the biggest carrot in the world?"

—Jilian S.

LUCKILY, THERE'S A WORLD CARROT MUSEUM TO help answer this, because there's more than one answer.

A:

The world's heaviest carrot ever weighed **20 POUNDS**. It was a twisted, weird mess that did not look tasty at all.

The world's longest carrot didn't look nearly as heavy, but it stretched a crazy **19 FEET 2 INCHES**.

How many heavy carrots would it take to weigh more than you?

Not that many.

If you weigh more than 20 pounds but less than 40, you need just

2 huge carrots.

If you weigh more than 40 pounds but less than 60, you need just

3 carrots.

If you weigh more than 60 pounds but less than 80, you need just

4 carrots,

and so on.

And how many of you would have to lie down end to end to match that 19-foot carrot?

• • • • • • •

If you're 4 feet 10 inches, keep adding that to itself:

4 feet 10 inches + 4 feet 10 inches = 8 feet 20 inches.

But 12 of those 20 inches make a new foot, so that's 9 feet 8 inches.

Not quite enough!

9 feet 8 inches + 4 feet 10 inches = 13 feet 18 inches or 14 feet 6 inches.

Still not enough.

14 feet 6 inches + 4 feet 10 inches = 18 feet 16 inches = 19 feet 4 inches.

Finally!

If you're around that height, we need 4 OF YOU to lie down end to end.

"How many breakfasts do I eat in my life?"

—Krista T.

BREAKFAST GIVES YOU ENERGY TO START THE day, so let's say you're eating it every day. It turns out there's a handy trick for guessing how often you do any daily activity:

Anything you do once a day, you do about 100 times every 3 months (because 3 × 30 = 90 and 3 × 31 days = 93 days) . . .

and about 1,000 times every 3 years (because 3 × 365 days = 1,095 days).

Using your age, you can figure out very quickly how often you do all kinds of things! For example, if you're 12 years old,

12 years ÷ 3 years = 4 sets of 1,000 days, so

A: a 12-year-old has eaten breakfast about 4,000 times.

IT'S BEEN SAID THAT AMERICA ORDERS 100 acres of pizza every day, which is about 75 football fields of pizza. An acre is 43,560 square feet, the same as a rectangle 66 feet wide and 660 feet long. If each pizza comes in an 18-inch (1½ feet) square box, we can find out how many boxes fit across that rectangle and from back to front.

66 feet ÷ 1½ feet per box = 44 boxes across

660 feet ÷ 1½ feet per box = 440 boxes front to back

So how many pizzas do we have in total?

44 rows × 440 pizzas in each row × 100 acres = 1,936,000 pizzas each day

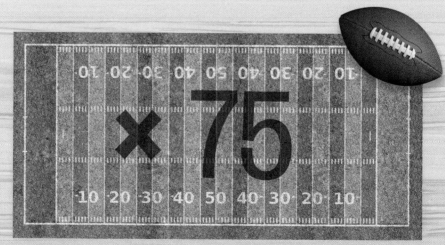

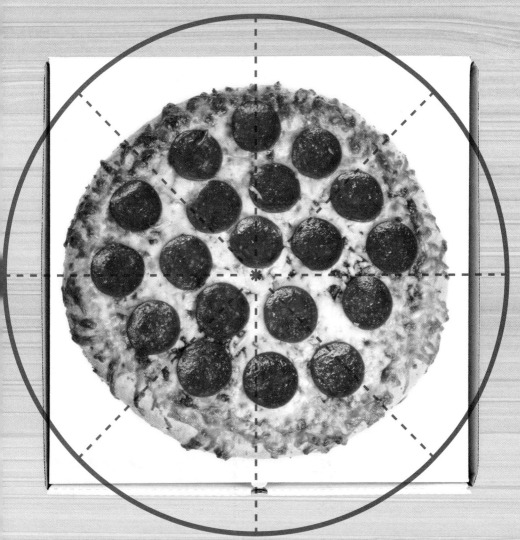

If there are 8 slices in each, that's

1,936,000 × 8 slices each = 15,488,000 slices each day.

So in 1 year we eat

15,488,000 slices each day × 365 days = 5,653,120,000 slices, or 5 BILLION PIECES OF PIZZA!

Q: "What's the biggest burger ever made?"

—Matt B.

A: As of the printing of this book, the biggest burger patty ever cooked weighed **6,040 POUNDS!** In 1999, folks in Saco, Montana, made the giant patty, which turned out to be **24 FEET WIDE.**

By the way, it took 2 hours to cook the burger on a specially made 576-square-foot grill.

How many people would it have taken to eat that thing?

If most people eat a quarter-pound patty, then it takes 4 people to eat 1 pound.

So 6,040 pounds × 4 people = 24,160 PEOPLE who could be fed by that one burger!

Let's hope someone brought enough ketchup.

"What's the fastest anyone can flip pancakes?"

—Lisa D.

THE WORLD RECORD SO FAR FOR TOSSING pancakes belongs to Chef Brad Jolly of Australia. In 2012, he flipped

140 pancakes in just 1 minute!

How many people could he have served breakfast to in that time?

· ·

If each person can eat a stack of 5 pancakes, then we find how many sets of 5 he flipped:

140 ÷ 5 = enough pancakes for 28 PEOPLE!

CHAPTER 4

YOUR LIFE IN NUMBERS

"How many pieces of gum can stick me to the wall and hold me there?"

—Joseph R.

FIRST WE NEED TO KNOW THE STICKINESS OF that gum. How many ounces or pounds can it hold up if it's stuck to the wall? Is the gum dried out enough to keep from stretching and letting you fall? We don't know exactly, but let's try to guess. If 1 piece of chewed-up gum is about as sticky as the backing for a picture hanger, the gum can hold up about 3 pounds.

3-pound picture frame

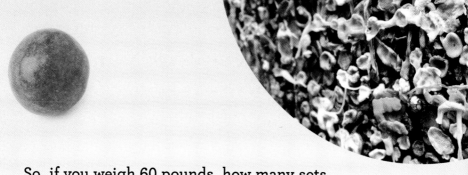

So, if you weigh 60 pounds, how many sets of 3 pounds add up to make you?

$60 \div 3 = 20$ sets

A:

So you'd need 20 pieces of gum.

"How many times do we blink while watching a movie?"

—Alexis V.

YOU MIGHT NOT EVEN NOTICE it, but every minute you're awake, you have to blink. Blinking keeps our eyes wet, pushes dust out of the way, and gives our brains quick, restful breaks from staring at stuff. To find the number of blinks during a movie, we need to know how many times we blink in 1 minute—and that depends on what we're doing. We normally blink 15 to 20 times per minute. But scientists have found that we blink less often when we're watching something interesting, like a movie. So let's say we drop to 10 blinks a minute.

An hour has 60 minutes.

So a 2-hour movie has 60 × 2 = 120 minutes.

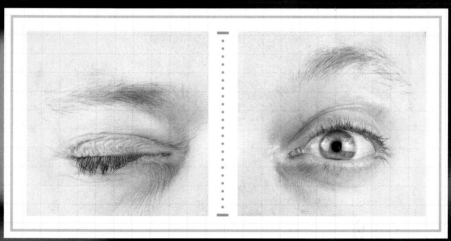

If we blink 10 times each minute, we get

A: 120 × 10 = **1,200 TIMES** we blink in a whole movie.

That means our minds will get 1,200 mininaps!

Q: "What is the longest jump rope someone used to jump rope?"

—Samantha D.

A: The longest jump rope ever skipped was more than **147 FEET LONG** and was jumped in 2011—but only 3 girls jumped it!

Far more people set the record for the most people jumping over one rope. In 2016, 300 people in Bangkok, Thailand, skipped together over the same rope 25 times! Even dogs have gotten into the act: 14 dogs from the Super Wan Wan Circus in Japan skipped rope together 16 times in 2013 to set their own jump rope world record.

Which group had more jumping feet or paws: the 300 people or the 14 dogs?

300 people × 2 feet each = 600 jumping feet

14 dogs × 4 paws each = 56 jumping paws

We would have needed 150 dogs to jump rope to match the people group . . . and a much longer rope.

"How many balloons would it take to carry me into the air?"

—Delilah B.

A PARTY BALLOON CAN LIFT THINGS ONLY IF it's filled with a gas that's lighter than air, like helium. Experts say that each liter of helium—which is about 1 quart—can lift 1 gram, which is metric for ⅟₂₈ of an ounce. (A regular-sized candy bar is about 2 ounces.) So, first we figure out how many grams a balloon can lift:

Here's a quick way to find the volume (the space taken up by something) of a ball: It takes up about ½ the volume of a cube that is the same width.

So if a balloon can fit in a box that's 1 foot long, wide, and tall, the balloon itself takes up about ½ a cubic foot of air.

A cubic foot fills the same space as about 28 liters, so that balloon holds about 14 liters of helium, meaning it can lift about 14 grams. Now find your weight in grams. For example, if you weigh about 50 pounds:

50 pounds × 16 ounces per pound = 800 ounces

800 ounces × 28 grams per ounce = about 22,000 grams

Now let's find how many
14-gram chunks you weigh:

22,000 grams ÷ 14 = 1,571

A: So it would take about
1,571 BALLOONS to
pick up a 50-pound kid.

Q: "How many words can you say in a day?"

—Simon G.

THERE'S A DIFFERENCE BETWEEN HOW MANY WE *can* say and how many we *do* say. Scientists have counted people's words and found that grown-ups say about 16,000 words in a day. But people spend some of the day chewing, or just breathing, or even snoring while sleeping. If you talked every single minute, you'd say more words. The speed record for talking is 655 words per minute. So if you talked at top speed the whole time you were awake, how many words would you say?

If you sleep 10 hours out of each 24-hour day, you're awake for 24 − 10 = 14 hours.

655 words per minute × 60 minutes in an hour = 39,300 words per hour

A: 39,300 words per hour × 14 hours awake = **550,200 WORDS IN A DAY**

16,000 words sounds like a lot less work.

"How fast do the balls travel in different sports, like tennis, soccer, baseball, lacrosse, and football?"

—Callie S.

THIS COMES DOWN TO A BASIC QUESTION: Can we throw a ball harder than we hit it? The math holds some surprises. For baseball, the fastest throws break the 100-mile-per-hour (mph) mark: Aroldis Chapman pitched a **105-MPH** fastball in 2010, and outfielder Aaron Hicks threw a ball at **105.5 MPH** in 2016! But the heavier the ball you throw with the same force, the slower the ball. A football weighs 14 to 15 ounces, compared with a 5-ounce baseball. Sure enough, the fastest football pass ever was a lot slower: Logan Thomas's **60-MPH** pass in 2014.

But using a bigger body part, or hitting the ball with an object, can make balls fly even faster. The fastest lacrosse shot clocked in just under **120 MPH** (Patrick Luehrsen in 2015). The fastest soccer kick flew at **131 MPH** (Ronny Heberson in 2006). The fastest tennis serves are all above 150 mph, with a record of **163.4 MPH** by Sam Groth in 2012. But the tiny golf ball rules: In 2013 Ryan Winther hit a golf ball at **217 MPH**!

If someone could throw a football as fast as that golf ball, how quickly would the ball fly from one end of the field all the way to the other end for a touchdown?

Between the end zones, a football field is 100 yards long. There are 3 feet in a yard, so that's

100 yards × 3 feet per yard = 300 feet.

We know that 15 miles per hour is exactly 22 feet per second. How many times as fast as that is 217 miles an hour?

217 mph ÷ 15 mph = 14½ times as fast.

So that golf ball is traveling about . . .

22 feet per second × 14½ = 319 feet per second.

Remember, we have 300 feet between the end zones.

The football would travel that whole length in less than 1 second!

Q: "Where do you spend more time, at school or at home?"

—Addison A.

YOU MIGHT FEEL LIKE SCHOOL TAKES UP your whole life, but the numbers tell us something else. You live 24 hours a day for 365 days a year, which comes to

$$24 \times 365 = 8{,}760 \text{ hours.}$$

If you sleep 10 hours a night, that comes to

$$10 \times 365 = 3{,}650 \text{ hours.}$$

So you're awake for only

$$8{,}760 - 3{,}650 = 5{,}110 \text{ hours.}$$

So how much of that do you spend in school? If you go to school 7 hours a day for 180 days a year, that comes to

7 × 180 = 1,260 hours.

And that's a small piece of the hours you're awake:

5,110 ÷ 1,260 = about 4.

A: You're in school only about ¼ of the time you're awake in 1 year!

Q: "When will I be a billion seconds old?"

—John O.

ONE BILLION SECONDS ISN'T AS FAR AWAY AS YOU think. Look at how many seconds you live in a year:

60 seconds each minute × 60 minutes each hour × 24 hours each day × 365 days each year = more than 31 million seconds (31,536,000)

So every 3 years, you live about 100 million seconds. You have to live only 10 times that long to live 1 billion seconds. But what exact day will it happen?

1,000,000,000 ÷ 31,536,000 = 31.709 years

Carve off the 31, then multiply the 0.709 by 12 to find out how many months that part is:

0.709 × 12 = 8.508 months

Now carve off those 8 months and multiply 0.508 times the 30 days in a month:

0.508 × 30 = 15.2 days

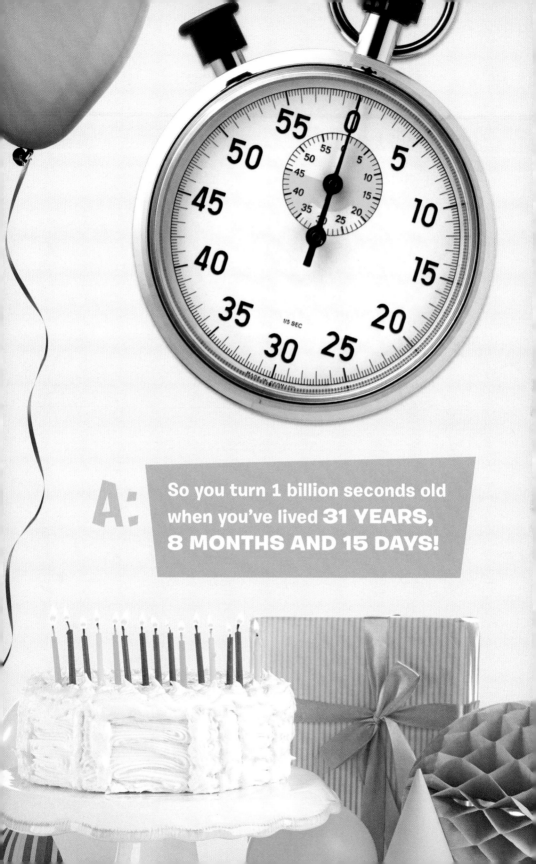

A: So you turn 1 billion seconds old when you've lived **31 YEARS, 8 MONTHS AND 15 DAYS!**

LAST NAMES HAVEN'T BEEN AROUND THAT LONG, compared with cavemen starting to use stone tools more than 2 million years ago.

A: People in England, for example, started using last names, or "surnames," after 1066, around 950 years ago.

What's crazy is that we have thousands of last names today in every country, but a few last names are shared by lots and lots of people. In America, almost 2½ million people are named Smith, and nearly 2 million are named Johnson. Together, the top 7 names (Smith, Johnson, Williams, Brown, Jones, Miller, and Davis) are shared by nearly 11 million people—about 1/30 of our whole country!

If a couple picks a last name and has 2 kids, each of whom gets married and has 2 kids with the same last name, and each of the grandkids does the same, and so do their kids, in 100 years, how many people in total will have had this last name?

• • • • • • • • • • •

At the start, just the 2 parents and the 2 kids have that name. 30 years later when the kids marry, if each couple keeps that last name, we now have the 2 parents in the older generation, plus 2 + 2 = 4 people in the next generation.

2 (parents) + 4 (kids and spouses) = 6 people

Then each of the 2 couples has 2 kids, giving us 4 grandkids total. Those 4 grandkids marry 30 years later. So at 60 years we have a new generation of 4 + 4 = 8 more people, and

6 (older people) + 8 (grandkids and spouses) = 14.

Then each of the 4 grandkid couples has 2 kids, for 8 kids total. If they all marry 30 years later, at 90 years we have

8 great-grandkids + 8 spouses = 16 people with the last name to add onto the pile.

14 (older people) + 16 (great-grandkids + spouses) = 30

As you see, every 30 years the new generation brings twice as many new kids, so we add the next multiple of 2: We added 4, then 8, then 16. In 100 years, 30 people have had that last name. In 300 years, we'll have added 10 generations, giving us

2 + 4 + 8 + 16 + 32 + 64 + 128 + 256 + 512 + 1,024 + 2,048 = 4,094 people.

That's way more than triple the 100-year number!

"How many cars can fit on a big highway at the same time?"

—Albert W.

THE FASTER CARS ARE DRIVING, THE FARTHER apart they have to be. That's because you need about 2 seconds to hit the brakes. The faster you're going, the farther you'll travel in that time. You need more space between you and the car in front of you. We know that 15 miles an hour is the same as 22 feet per second. But cars on the highway drive about 60 miles per hour. To find out how many times as fast 60 is compared to 15:

$60 ÷ 15 = 4$

That means 60 mph is 4 times as fast as 15 mph.

So 22 feet per second × 4 = 88 feet per second.

88 × 2 seconds = 176 feet needed between cars to pass that point 2 seconds later.

Cars themselves are about 15 feet long, so each car plus the space behind it takes up

$176 + 15 = 191$ feet.

How many of those fit in 1 mile? A mile has 5,280 feet, so

5,280 feet ÷ 191 = about 28 cars.

So on a 4-lane highway, 28 cars × 4 lanes = 112 cars fit in every mile.

And since 60 of those mile-long chains of cars pass by every hour,

A: 112 × 60 = **6,720 CARS.**

What's the greatest number of cars that can pass by? Remember, if they're driving slowly, they're packed closer together, but not many cars pass by each minute. Faster cars have to spread farther apart. At any speed, it's about 1 car every 2 seconds per lane—but don't forget, the car itself has a length. In his book *Traffic*, expert Tom Vanderbilt found that 55 to 60 miles per hour is the perfect speed to pump the most cars through a highway.

Q: "How many times would the wheels of our car have to turn to travel all the way around the world once?"

—Thompson T.

DIFFERENT CARS HAVE DIFFERENT SIZE TIRES. BUT they all turn, and they can all take you around the world (if you could drive on water). Car tires are about 26 to 28 inches wide in total. To find the distance around the tire—the circumference—we multiply the diameter times pi (that's 3.14). (See "A Bite of Pi," p. 2.) For a tire 28 inches across,

28 × 3.14 = about 88 inches. That's how far you drive in 1 tire turn.

Now let's find out how many turns you need per mile:

A mile has 5,280 feet.

88 inches

25,000 miles

5,280 feet × 12 inches in each foot = 63,360 inches

63,360 inches ÷ 88 inches per tire turn = 720 tire turns

And to drive the 25,000 miles around our planet,

25,000 × 720 = 18,000,000.

A: Your wheels would have to turn 18 million times to drive around Earth!

CHAPTER 5

EARTH AND FRIENDS

"What happens if you dig a hole straight down into the ground? How far until you reach the bottom?"

—Ajax L.

IT DEPENDS WHAT YOU MEAN BY "THE BOTTOM." IF you want to dig to the center of the earth, it's about 3,958 miles to the very middle. But if you want to dig all the way through, it's

3,958 + 3,958 = 7,916 miles to the other side.

How did we get that using only mental math?

3,958 is the same as 3,000 + 900 + 50 + 8.

So to double 3,958, we double each of those pieces, then add them up:

3,000 × 2 = 6,000

900 × 2 = 1,800

50 × 2 = 100

8 × 2 = 16

Then you get 6,000 + 1,800 = 7,800.

7,800 + 100 = 7,900

7,900 + 16= 7,916

3,958 miles

A: The crazy thing is, the deepest that humans have ever dug is just 7½ miles, or less than ⅟₁₀₀₀ of the way across! But if you want to dig deeper, just remember that the center of Earth is a 10,000-degree blob of iron and nickel. You'll need a superpowerful heat suit.

"If you took the plastic bottles used in 1 day and wrapped them around the earth, how many times would they wrap around?"

—Carter F.

EARTH MIGHT BE A TINY LITTLE BALL compared to all of space, but it's huge compared to us. If you measure around its widest point, it's about 25,000 miles around! Every mile has many, many feet, so that's a lot of plastic bottles. But we use a lot of plastic bottles; America alone uses about 50 billion water bottles a year. If each bottle is 1 foot tall, how far can they stretch?

50,000,000,000 water bottles in a year ÷ 365 days in a year = about 137,000,000 water bottles in a day

Earth is 25,000 miles × 5,280 feet in each mile = 132,000,000 feet around.

A: So if water bottles are about 1 foot tall, they wrap around the earth once and then some!

We use bottles for other kinds of drinks, too. If we included those, they would wrap around many times more.

"How many people would it take to hold hands and circle the earth?"

—Tori O.

NOW THAT WE KNOW FROM THE LAST QUESTION the distance around the earth (132,000,000 feet), here's another cool fact: Your arm span is about the same as your height. If people average 5½ feet tall, then they can stretch their arms 5½ feet across. So let's find out how many sets of 5½ fit in 132,000,000 feet.

A: 132,000,000 feet ÷ 5½ feet per person = **24,000,000 PEOPLE,** or about ¹⁄₁₂ the population of the United States!

Q: "How long would it take to run around the world?"

—Valeria S.

SINCE WE KNOW THAT EARTH IS 25,000 miles around, we can figure out how long it takes to travel that far. A healthy grown-up can run about 6 miles an hour. So if we're awake 14 hours daily and run nonstop, how far can we run in a day?

6 miles each hour × 14 hours each day = 84 miles a day

Then we find out how many 84-mile sections we have to run:

 A: 25,000 miles ÷ 84 miles = about **297 DAYS** to run around the world (if you could run on water, too!)

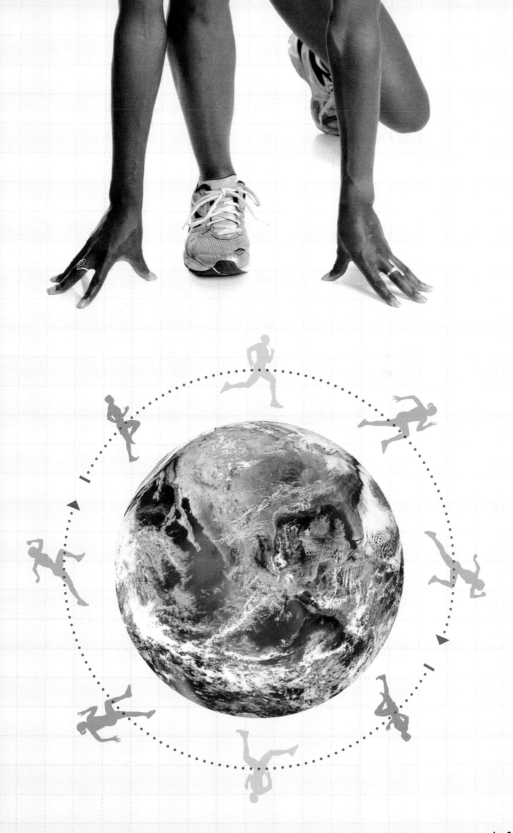

"How many 1-inch-by-1-inch puzzle pieces would it take to cover Earth?"

—Bailey H.

IF YOU THINK 25,000 MILES AROUND THE earth sounds like a long trip, imagine the area that covers Earth! Earth is about 8,000 miles across at its widest point, so

4 × pi (that's 3.14) × 4,000 × 4,000 = about 200,000,000 (200 million) square miles.

(See "A Bite of Pi," p. 2.)

Each square mile contains 5,280 rows of 5,280 1-foot-wide squares, so

5,280 × 5,280 = about 28,000,000 square feet in each square mile.

And each square foot contains 12 rows of 12 little inch-wide squares:

12 × 12 = 144 square inches in each square foot.

So those 200,000,000 square miles contain

200,000,000 × 28,000,000 square feet in each square mile × 144 square inches in each square foot =

A: 806,400,000,000,000,000, or more than 800 *quadrillion* puzzle pieces!

"How many soccer balls would fit inside a hollow Earth?"

—Alex and Jacob W.

BALLS AND BOXES LOOK DIFFERENT, but the space inside them follows the same math trick. If you have a perfect cube that's twice the size of another cube in all three directions (across, back to front, and top to bottom), it will hold 2 × 2 × 2 as much space, or 8 times as much. Same with a ball: If you double its width, it holds 8 times as much space. If you make it 10 times as wide, its space is 10 × 10 × 10 = 1,000 times as much!

So how does a soccer ball compare with Earth? World Cup soccer balls are about 9 inches wide, or ¾ of a foot. Meanwhile, Earth is 8,000 *miles* across. So we find how many times as wide Earth is:

¾ foot

1 mile has 5,280 feet.

8,000 miles × 5,280 = 42,240,000 feet

42,240,000 ÷ ¾ feet = 56,320,000 times as wide as a soccer ball

Then we multiply that number by itself, then by itself again . . . which means Earth takes up 56,320,000 × 56,320,000 × 56,320,000 =

178,640,000,000,000,000,000,000 **as much space as a soccer ball!**

When you pack balls, though, they don't squish to fill every bit of space; they leave about ¼ of it empty. So we can fit ¾ as many soccer balls as that, which gives us

8,000 miles

A:

178,640,000,000,000,000,000,000 x ¾ = 133,980,000,000,000,000,000,000 balls!

That's 133 *sextillion* soccer balls: a million times a million times a million times another 133,980.

Q: **"How many tennis balls would it take to fill the moon?"**

—Logan L.

O N THE LAST PAGE, WE ALREADY ANSWERED THIS question without knowing it! It turns out the moon holds about the same number of tennis balls as the Earth holds soccer balls. Why is that? The moon is 2,000 miles wide, compared to 8,000 for Earth. If you smushed the moon against the United States, it would stretch from Jacksonville, Florida, to San Diego, California. Since the moon is ¼ as wide as Earth, it holds

¼ × ¼ × ¼ = 1/64 as much stuff as Earth.

But a tennis ball is also about ¼ the width of a soccer ball, so each one takes up ¼ × ¼ × ¼ or 1/64 as much space. So . . .

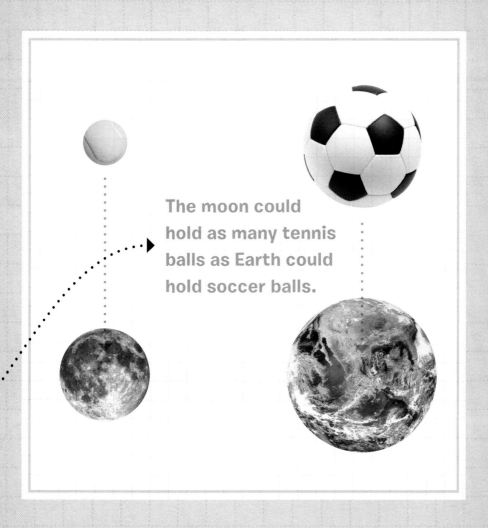

The moon could hold as many tennis balls as Earth could hold soccer balls.

A: **133,980,000,000,000,000,000,000 tennis balls.**

That's too many to count in a lifetime.

Q: "How many ladders would it take to get me to the moon?"

—Evelyn L.

OUR MOON SAILS AROUND EARTH FROM 240,000 miles away. If your ladders stretch 8 feet each, we need the number of 8-foot chunks between us and the moon:

240,000 miles × 5,280 feet in each mile = 1,267,200,000 . . . about 1 billion feet

A: 1,267,200,000 ÷ 8 feet per ladder = 158,400,000. So you'd need more than **158 MILLION LADDERS** to get there!

By the way, here's another cool fact: If you lined up all 7 of the other planets in our solar system next to each other, they would fill about the same distance as between Earth and the moon!

The same distance between Earth and the moon!

Earth

Mercury
3,032 miles

Venus
7,521 miles

Mars
4,221 miles

Jupiter
88,846 miles

If the planets line up side by side and we add up their widths,

3,032 + 7,521 + 4,221 + 88,846 + 74,897 + 31,763 + 30,755 = 241,035 miles!

(Planets are not shown exactly to scale.)

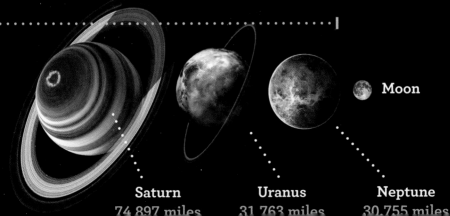

Moon

Saturn
74,897 miles

Uranus
31,763 miles

Neptune
30,755 miles

"How many times does Earth go around the sun in a year?"

—Ruby Mae C.

IT DEPENDS WHOSE YEAR YOU'RE TALKING ABOUT!

A: An Earth year is the time it takes us to go around the sun once.

But in that time, the planet Mercury goes around the sun more than 4 times, since it takes only 88 of our days. If you've been living on Mercury (without burning up in the 1,000-degree sunshine), you're more than 4 times as many years old as you are here on Earth!

So how many years old are you on other planets?

In our year, Mars goes only about halfway around the sun. It takes 687 of our days to make the trip, nearly 2 years. So on Mars, you're only ½ as many years old.

If you're 8 years old here, Martians think you're only 4 of their years.

Jupiter takes nearly 12 of our years to go around the sun. So you'd be ¹⁄₁₂ as old. However many years old you are, you're just that many months old on Jupiter!

A 10-year-old here is only 10 months old to a Jupiter resident.

And way out there, Neptune takes 164 of our years. For every year you've lived here, it's just $\frac{1}{164}$ of a year to them . . . what we would call about 2 $\frac{1}{5}$ days.

So a 10-year-old Earthling is only 25 days old on Neptune.

Q: "How big is the sun? How many Earths could fit inside the sun?"

—Elijah B.

THE SUN IN OUR SKY IS REALLY A STAR. EVEN though it's really hot—a million degrees in some parts—it's 93 million miles away, far enough so it doesn't burn us to a crisp.

Here's a quick way to remember how big the sun is: The planet Jupiter is roughly 10 times as wide as Earth, and the sun is about 10 times as wide as Jupiter! So the sun is

10 × 10 = about 100 times as wide as Earth (The sun is 864,000 miles wide and Earth is 8,000 miles wide).

Just as we found out how many soccer balls squeeze inside Earth (see p. 106), we can find how many Earths could squish inside the sun: If the sun is 100 times as wide, 100 times as tall, and 100 times as deep, it holds . . .

100 × 100 × 100 as much space, which is 1,000,000 times as much space.

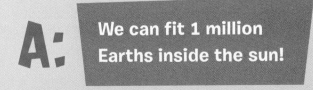
A: We can fit 1 million Earths inside the sun!

"Assuming you could survive the heat, how long would it take to orbit the sun in a spacecraft?"

—Sebastian B.

IT DEPENDS HOW FAR FROM THE SUN YOU ARE flying. You have to fly fast enough not to fall into the sun (because of gravity) but slow enough not to shoot off into space. If you're flying 93 million miles from the sun, as Earth does, you'll take 1 year, just like Earth—because Earth is like a spaceship itself. But if you fly really close, say at ¹⁄₁₀₀ that distance, you'll have to fly around the sun in ¹⁄₁₀₀₀ of the time Earth takes. How much time will that take?

We have 365 days in our year, with 24 hours in each:

365 × 24 = 8,760 hours in a year

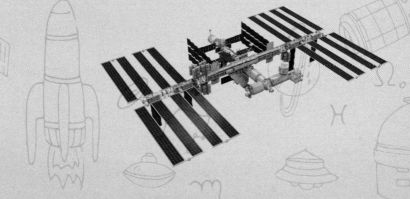

864,000
miles

If the spaceship takes ¹⁄₁₀₀₀ of that, we get

8,760 ÷ 1,000 = 8.76 hours

A: Your spacecraft will take **less than 9 hours** to go around!

Q: "How long would it take to travel to Pluto?"

—Victoria and Emilia I.

WE KNOW EXACTLY HOW LONG IT TAKES A spaceship to reach Pluto, because we've sent one—but without people on board. The New Horizons spacecraft took 9 years to fly more than 3 *billion* miles to Pluto. In July 2015 it whizzed past Pluto and snapped amazing photos. That's a long trip!

How fast did New Horizons fly?

9 years × 365 days per year × 24 hours per day = about 79,000 hours

3,000,000,000 miles ÷ 79,000 hours = 38,000 miles per hour!

A plane flying 1,000 miles an hour would take 38 times as long, or **342 YEARS**.

CHAPTER 6

NOW DO IT IN YOUR HEAD!

7 SLICK TRICKS TO AMAZE YOUR FRIENDS

Multiply by 5 at Top Speed

IF YOU HAVE 5 OF SOMETHING, THAT'S ½ AS MUCH as having 10 of them. So a fast way to multiply by 5 is to multiply by 10, then cut the number in ½ —or better yet, take ½ of it first, then multiply by 10 by tacking on a zero. Let's try it:

What's 24 × 5?

½ of 24 is 12.

Tack on a zero.

The answer is 120.

Let's try it with 68! Take ½ of 68 to get 34, tack a zero onto the end . . . that's right,

68 × 5 = 340.

Multiply by 11

11 IS A REALLY FUN NUMBER. WHEN YOU HAVE 11 of something, you take 10 of them and add on one more. For 2-digit numbers, this makes a cute pattern. Let's look at 35 × 11:

35 × 10 = 350

$$\begin{array}{r} 350 \\ + 35 \\ \hline 385 \end{array}$$

You see what happened there? The middle digit (8) is just the first and second digits from your starting number (3 and 5) added together. This works for any 2-digit number: Add the digits, then shove the sum into the middle of the number, and you get that number times 11!

Let's try it with 62 × 11:

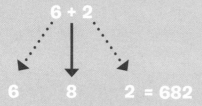

6   8   2 = 682

One more thing: If the digits add up to 10 or more, you take the 1 and add it to the first digit. So 75 × 11:

7 [7 + 5 = 12] 5

Add that 1 from the 12 to the 7 to get the correct answer of 825 (not 7,125).

Pop Out Perfect Squares

A PERFECT SQUARE HAPPENS WHEN YOU MULTIPLY A number by itself, because that gives you the area of a square that wide. We know

$$1 × 1 = 1, \ 2 × 2 = 4, \ 3 × 3 = 9, \ 4 × 4 = 16 \ldots$$

Do you notice anything about the gaps between these squares?

This goes on forever. Just keep adding the next odd number, and you'll get the next perfect square! 16 + 9 = 25 (which is 5 × 5), 25 + 11 = 36 (which is 6 × 6), and so on.

What else do you notice about the odd number you add on? It's the sum of the square roots (the small numbers you started with) of the two squares it sits between.

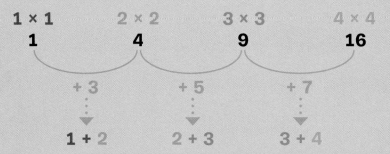

So to get from 9 (3 × 3) to 16 (4 × 4), you just add 3, then 4.

$$9 + 3 + 4 = 9 + 7 = 16$$

So if you want to be a show-off, and you know that 16 × 16 is 256, you can instantly figure out 17 × 17:

$$256 + 16 + 17 = 289.$$

NOW LET'S SQUARE SOME NUMBERS TO GET REALLY big answers. Any 2-digit number that ends in 5 has a really cool trick: Just take the first digit, multiply it by the next digit up, then tack on a 25 to the number you get, and you have your answer!

Let's try it with 25 × 25:

1 more than 2 is 3:

2 × 3 = 6

Then tack on a 25, and you get 625:

25 × 25 = 625

Try to find the square of 65:

6 × 7 = 42

Tack on the 25, and you get **4,225**.

That's the answer to 65 × 65!

Slice and Dice

WHEN YOU'RE ASKED TO DIVIDE A NUMBER BY 3, 7, or 9, there's a handy trick for each that helps you figure out whether the numbers divide nice and neatly.

Any multiple of 3 has digits that add up to a multiple of 3.

So for 21, 2 + 1 = 3, so the answer is yes (21 is in fact 3 × 7).

For a bigger number like 4,317, we add 4 + 3 + 1 + 7 = 15, which is a multiple of 3 (since 1 + 5 = 6, which is a multiple, too).

Sure enough, 4,317 is 3 × 1,439.

This works for the number 9 as well: Just add the digits, and for any multiple of 9 they'll add up to a multiple of 9. So 4,317 is not a multiple of 9—it adds up to 15, which isn't a multiple of 9. But 4,320 is, because 4 + 3 + 2 + 0 = 9.

It gets a little fancier with 7. You take the last digit, double it, and subtract from the rest of the number without that digit on there. If the answer is a multiple of 7, so is the original number.

Take 154: split off the 4 to leave 15.

4 × 2 = 8

15 − 8 = 7

Yes! 154 is 7 × 22.

Go Triangular

IF YOU'VE EVER STACKED CUPS OR WATCHED cheerleaders stack themselves, you know that only some numbers can make a pyramid:

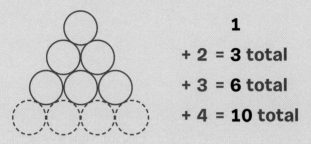

$$
\begin{array}{l}
1 \\
+\ 2 = \textbf{3 total} \\
+\ 3 = \textbf{6 total} \\
+\ 4 = \textbf{10 total}
\end{array}
$$

If you keep going and add 5, then 6, then 7, and so on, you get the numbers called *triangle numbers*: 1, 3, 6, 10, 15, 21. . . . And the cool thing is, you can find the total number in any triangle just by knowing how many objects are in the bottom row.

That triangle is ½ the area of a rectangle that is just as tall, but 1 thing wider. So a triangle with 6 things on the bottom covers ½ the area of a rectangle that is 6 units tall and 7 units wide (7 is 1 more than 6).

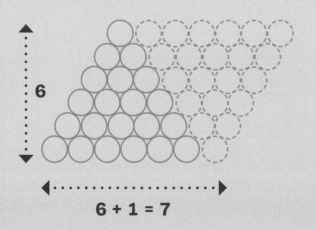

6

6 + 1 = 7

6 × 7 = 42 = the area of that rectangle. The triangle covers ½ of that, so

42 ÷ 2 = 21.

A triangle that stacks 1, 2, 3, 4, 5, and 6 things will have 21 things in total.

Seal It with a Handshake

THESE TRIANGLE NUMBERS SHOW UP EVERYWHERE, not just in stacking things. If 6 people all shake hands so everyone shakes hands with everyone else exactly once, how many handshakes happen?

Each ball is a person, and each line is a handshake.

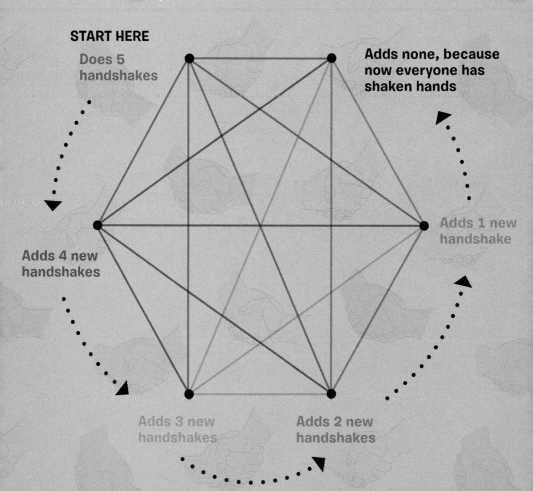

START HERE

Does 5 handshakes

Adds none, because now everyone has shaken hands

Adds 1 new handshake

Adds 4 new handshakes

Adds 3 new handshakes

Adds 2 new handshakes

The first person shakes hands with 5 people (everyone but herself).

The next person has only 4 people left to shake hands with.

The third person has only 3 people left.

The fourth person has only 2 people left.

The fifth person has only 1 more person.

The last person adds no new handshakes, since he already got counted when he shook hands with person #1, person #2, and so on.

So 5 + 4 + 3 + 2 + 1 = 15 handshakes happen.

It's the triangle number for 5, which is one less than 6. The pattern works for any size group. If 21 people shake hands, you need the triangle number for 20. (See Go Triangular on p. 127.)

20 × (20 + 1) = 420

420 ÷ 2 = 210 handshakes will happen.

Now you can take your tricks and wow your friends!

SOURCES

CHAPTER 1: ANIMAL MATH

"HOW MANY GUINEA PIGS CAN FIT ON A PLANE?" —ANDREW L.

Guinea pig law:
http://www.spiegel.de/international/zeitgeist/hope-for-lonely-rodents-rent-a-guinea-pig-service-takes-off-in-switzerland-a-787336.html

Guinea pig length: Author measured own pets.

Airplane volume:
https://www.quora.com/How-many-ping-pong-balls-can-fit-into-a-747

"HOW MANY BIRDS WOULD IT TAKE TO PICK YOU UP AND FLY WITH YOU?" —KAIEN M.

San Diego Zoo Animals. "Harpy Eagle," last modified 2016, http://animals.sandiegozoo.org/animals/harpy-eagle.

Schulenberg, T. S., ed. 2009. "Harpy Eagle (*Harpia harpyja*)," Neotropical Birds Online. Ithaca: Cornell Lab of Ornithology, 2009. Retrieved from Neotropical Birds Online: http://neotropical.birds.cornell.edu/portal/species/overview?p_p_spp=20613.

"HOW MANY BEES DOES IT TAKE TO MAKE ONE JAR OF HONEY?" —NINA J.

Palermo, Elizabeth. "What is Honey?" Live Science, June 20, 2013, http://www.livescience.com/37611-what-is-honey-honeybees.html.

Tan, Ruth. "20 Amazing Honey Bee Facts!" Benefits of Honey, http://www.benefits-of-honey.com/honey-bee-facts.html.

Turnbull, Bill. "Ask a Grown-Up: How Do Bees Make Honey?" *The Guardian*, August 10, 2013, http://www.theguardian.com/lifeandstyle/2013/aug/10/how-bees-make-honey-ask-a-grown-up.

"HOW MANY TWIGS ARE IN A BIRD'S NEST?" —SOPHIE O.

Annenberg Learner. "Building a Robin Nest," American Robin Kids, Journey North, https://www.learner.org/jnorth/tm/robin/BuildNest.html.

Campbell, Bruce, and Elizabeth Lack, eds. *A Dictionary of Birds*. Carlton, England: T and AD Poyser, 1985.

Goodfellow, Peter. *Avian Architecture: How Birds Design, Engineer, and Build*. Princeton, NJ: Princeton University Press, 2011.

National Eagle Center. "Bald Eagle Nesting and Young," http://www.baldeagleinfo.com/eagle/eagle4.html.

"HOW MANY SPIDERS ARE THERE IN THE WHOLE WORLD?" —CHARLIE Y.

Buddle, Chris. "You Are Always Within Three Feet of a Spider: Fact or Fiction?" Arthropod Ecology, June 5, 2012, https://arthropodecology.com/2012/06/05/you-are-always-within-three-feet-of-a-spider-fact-or-fiction.

Szalay, Jessie. "Types of Spiders & Spider Facts," Live Science, November 4, 2014, http://www.livescience.com/22122-types-of-spiders.html.

"HOW MANY DOGS ARE THERE IN THE WHOLE WORLD?" —KAIYA AND KEIRY R.

Companion Animal Responsible Ownership. "Statistics on Dogs," www.carodog.eu/statistics-on-cats-and-dogs.

Coren, Stanley. "How Many Dogs Are There in the World?," *Psychology Today*, September 19, 2012, https://www.psychologytoday.com/blog/canine-corner/201209/how-many-dogs-are-there-in-the-world.

Humane Society of the United States. "Pets by the Numbers," www.humanesociety.org/issues/pet_overpopulation/facts/pet _ownership_statistics.html.

. . . .

"IF A LADYBUG WERE ME-SIZED, HOW MANY DOTS WOULD IT HAVE?" —LUCY P.

Weill Medical College of Cornell University. "Body Surface Area," Pediatric Critical Care, www-users.med.cornell.edu/~spon/picu/calc/ bsacalc.htm.

. . . .

"HOW MANY TEETH DOES A KOMODO DRAGON HAVE?" —WILL F.

Helfman, Gene, and George H. Burgess, *Sharks*. Baltimore: Johns Hopkins University Press, 2014, pp. 29–30.

Layton, Julia. "Are Komodo Dragons' Mouths Deadlier Than Cobras' Venom?" HowStuffWorks.com, July 8, 2008, animals.howstuffworks.com /animal-facts/komodo-bite1.htm.

McElhatton, Ann. "Sink Your Teeth into This: 20 Facts About Shark Teeth," Beach Chair Scientist, August 12, 2012, beachchairscientist.com /2012/08/12/sink-your-teeth-into-this-20-facts-about-shark-teeth.

. . . .

"HOW LONG DOES IT TAKE A DEER TO GROW ANTLERS?" —EMERSON B.

Salwey, Mary Kay. "Amazing Antlers: Fast-Growing Bone a Seasonal Phenomena," Alaska Department of Fish and Game, November 2005, http://www.adfg.alaska.gov/index.cfm?adfg=wildlifenews.view _article&articles_id=175.

. . . .

"IF I WERE AS STRONG AS AN ANT, HOW MUCH COULD I PICK UP?" —SOPHIA Y.

AntAsk. "How can ants carry so much weight?," *AntBlog*, October 5, 2012, www.antweb.org/antblog/2012/10/how-can-ants-carry-so-much- weight-nathalie-france.html.

BBC. "Leaf-Cutter Ants," *Nature Wildlife*, October 2014, www.bbc.co.uk/ nature/life/Atta_%28genus%29#intro.

Hattam, Jennifer. "Ant Weight-Lifting 'Champ' Hoists 100x Its Own Weight," *Treehugger*, February 21, 2010, www.treehugger.com/natural- sciences/ant-weight-lifting-champ-hoists-100x-its-own-weight.html.

National Geographic. "Asian Elephant (*Elephas maximus*)," www.nationalgeographic.com/animals/mammals/a/asian-elephant.

Skinner, J. D., and Christian T. Chimimba. *The Mammals of the Southern African Subregion*, 3rd ed. Cambridge: Cambridge University Press, 2005, p. 617.

Wildscreen Arkive. "Indian Rhinoceros," www.arkive.org.

. . . .

"HOW MANY TIMES DO DOGS TAKE BATHS IN A YEAR?" —JOVIANNE S.

Kam, Katherine. "Pet Health: Why Bathing and Brushing Are Important," *WebMD Healthy Pets*, May 7, 2013, pets.webmd.com/features/pets-bathe -groom-important.

. . . .

"WHAT MOVES FASTER, A HOPPING BUNNY OR A RUNNING PERSON?" —INAYA K.

International Association of Athletics Federations. "100 Metres Men All Time Best," www.iaaf.org/records/toplists/sprints/100-metres/outdoor /men/senior.

National Geographic. "Eastern Cottontail Rabbit," www.nationalgeographic.com/animals/mammals/e/eastern-cottontail -rabbit.

National Geographic. "Black-Tailed Jackrabbit," www.nationalgeographic.com/animals/mammals/b/black-tailed -jackrabbit.

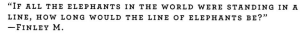

"IF ALL THE ELEPHANTS IN THE WORLD WERE STANDING IN A LINE, HOW LONG WOULD THE LINE OF ELEPHANTS BE?" —FINLEY M.

International Union for the Conservation of Nature. "Provisional African Elephant Population Estimates," Elephant Database, December 31, 2013, www.elephantdatabase.org/preview_report/2013_africa_final/2013 /Africa.

World Wide Fund for Nature. "Asian Elephants," wwf.panda.org /what_we_do/endangered_species/elephants/asian_elephants.

CHAPTER 2: NATURE GONE WILD

"HOW FAST DOES THE FASTEST TREE IN THE WORLD GROW?" —MIHIRA AND SIONA T.

Cornell University. "Mowing," www.gardening.cornell.edu /homegardening/sceneec8a.html.

Guinness World Records. "Fastest Growing Tree," January 1, 2011, www .guinnessworldrecords.com/world-records/fastest-growing-tree-.

Innes, Robin J. 2009. *Paulownia tomentosa*. In: Fire Effects Information System, [Online]. U.S. Department of Agriculture, Forest Service, Rocky Mountain Research Station, Fire Sciences Laboratory (Producer), http:// www.fs.fed.us/database/feis/plants/tree/pautom/all.html.

Reference. "How fast does grass grow?" www.reference.com/ home-garden/fast-grass-grow-6555526ab6032e3a.

"HOW MANY STATES IN THE U.S. HAVE SNOW?" —CARRIE S.

Current Results. "Average Yearly Snowfall by American State," www .currentresults.com/Weather/US/average-snowfall by state.php.

Current Results. "Average Annual Snowfall in Alabama," www .currentresults.com/Weather/Alabama/annual-snowfall.php.

Osborn, Liz. "Snowiest Places in United States," Current Results, www .currentresults.com/Weather-Extremes/US/snowiest.php.

"HOW MANY SPIDER WEBS DOES IT TAKE TO WEIGH THE SAME AMOUNT AS A BANANA?" —EVERETT V.

Ko, Frank K., et al. "Engineering Properties of Spider Silk," web.mit.edu /course/3/3.064/www/slides/Ko_spider_silk.pdf.

Wikipedia, s.v. "Spider Silk," last modified June 7, 2016, en.wikipedia .org/wiki/Spider_silk.

"HOW MANY LEAVES ARE ON A WHOLE TREE?" —EMILY T.

Living Tree Educational Foundation. "Tree Facts," 2010, www.livingtreeeducationalfoundation.org/tree_facts.html.

Warnell School of Forestry and Natural Resources. "Assessing Soil Water Resource Space: Tree Soil Water Method," Trees and Water Series, University of Georgia, May 2012, https://www.warnell.uga.edu/index.php /outreach/publications/individual/assessing-soil-water-resource-space -tree-soil-water-.

"HOW FAR ARE THE CLOUDS FROM US?" —ANOUSHKA M.

Ackerman, Steven A., and Jonathan Martin. "How Fast Do Raindrops Fall?" The Weather Guys, September 10, 2013, wxguys.ssec.wisc .edu/2013/09/10/how-fast-do-raindrops-fall.

Met Office. "Clouds," www.metoffice.gov.uk/learning/clouds.

"HOW MANY LIGHTBULBS COULD I LIGHT UP WITH A WINDMILL

ON MY ROOF?" —TALIE B.

Iowa Energy Center. "Wind Speed and Power," http://www
.iowaenergycenter.org/wind-energy-manual/wind-and-wind-power
/wind-speed-and-power.

. . . .

"WHICH WIND BLOWS FASTER, A TORNADO OR A HURRICANE?"
—CAROLYN L.

Accuracy Tech. "How to Read the Wind – The Ultimate Guide," June 25,
2015, www.accuracy-tech.com/how-to-read-the-wind-the-ultimate
-guide-3.

Australia Government, Bureau of Meteorology. "Tropical Cyclone Olivia,"
April 1996, http://www.bom.gov.au/cyclone/history/wa/olivia.shtml.

National Ocean Service. "What is the difference between a hurricane, a
cyclone, and a typhoon?," www.oceanservice.noaa.gov/facts/cyclone
.html.

National Weather Service Weather Forecast Office. "Beaufort Wind Scale,"
www.srh.noaa.gov/mfl/?n=beaufort.

Royal Meteorological Society. "Beaufort Scale," www.rmets.org
/weather-and-climate/observing/beaufort-scale.

Williams, Jack. "Doppler Radar Measures 318 mph Wind in Tornado,"
USA Today, May 17, 2005, usatoday30.usatoday.com/weather/tornado
/wtwur318.htm.

. . . .

"HOW MANY GALLONS OF WATER DOES IT TAKE TO PUT OUT A
FIRE?" —SELAH AND ABI H.

Pennsylvania Department of Environmental Protection. "Color Scheme for
Identifying the Capacity of Fire Hydrants," Drinking Water and Wastewater
Operator Information Center, www.dep.state.pa.us/dep/deputate/
waterops/redesign/TablesNFormulas/Pages/firehydrantcolor.htm.

Stump, Derek. "So You Wanna Be a . . . Firefighter," Bedtime Math,
January 24, 2014, bedtimemath.org/fighting-fire-with-numbers.

. . . .

CHAPTER 3: MATH FOR YOUR MOUTH

"WHAT WOULD 85 POUNDS (MY WEIGHT) OF CHOCOLATE LOOK
LIKE ON THE COCOA PLANT?" —RYAN AND DYLAN T.

Amano Artisan Chocolate. "How Many Cocoa Beans Are in a Pod?," www
.amanochocolate.com/faqs/how-many-cocoa-beans-are-in-a-pod.

Cadbury. "Harvesting and Processing Cocoa Beans," www.cadbury.com
.au/about-chocolate/harvesting-and-processing-cocoa-beans.aspx.

Cook, L. Russell. "Cacao Tree," *Encyclopedia Britannica*, www.britannica
.com/plant/cacao.

Moore Jr., Scott. "How Many Cocoa Beans Are in a Chocolate Bar?"
Tejas Chocolate Craftory, June 5, 2013, tejaschocolate.com/how-many
-cocoa-beans-are-in-a-chocolate-bar.

Scharffenberger. "The Cacao Plant," www.scharffenberger.com/our-story
/about-cacao/cacao-plant.

. . . .

"HOW MUCH CHOCOLATE DOES THE AVERAGE PERSON EAT EACH
DAY? AND IF I EAT 15 TIMES THAT, HOW MUCH CHOCOLATE DO I
EAT IN A YEAR?" —JILLIAN T.

McCarthy, Niall. "The World's Biggest Chocolate Consumers," *Forbes*,
July 22, 2015, www.forbes.com/sites/niallmccarthy/2015/07/22/
the-worlds-biggest-chocolate-consumers-infographic/#516a145712b8.

. . . .

"ABOUT HOW MUCH FOOD DO WE EAT EVERY DAY?" —VASILY M.

Andrews, Ryan. "What are your 4 pounds made of?," Precision Nutrition,
www.precisionnutrition.com/what-are-your-4-lbs.

Aubrey, Alison. "The Average American Ate (Literally) a Ton This Year," December 31, 2011, National Public Radio, www.npr.org/sections/thesalt /2011/12/31/144478009/the-average-american-ate-literally-a-ton -this-year.

Quilty-Harper, Conrad. "The world's fattest countries: how do you compare?," June 21, 2012, *The Telegraph*, www.telegraph.co.uk/news /earth/earthnews/9345086/The-worlds-fattest-countries-how-do-you -compare.html.

San Diego Zoo. "Mammals: Elephant," animals.sandiegozoo.org/animals /elephant.

San Diego Zoo. "Mammals: Giraffe," animals.sandiegozoo.org/animals /giraffe.

San Diego Zoo. "Mammals: Hippo," animals.sandiegozoo.org/animals /hippo.

"WHAT'S THE BIGGEST CARROT IN THE WORLD?" —JILIAN S.

World Carrot Museum. "The World Record Carrot Growers—Heaviest and Longest," www.carrotmuseum.co.uk/record.html.

"HOW MANY PIECES OF PIZZA ARE EATEN IN THE U.S. EACH YEAR?" —DEVIN S.

Dickson, Caitlin. "100 Acres of Pizza Served Daily in the U.S.," June 21, 2011, *The Atlantic*, http://www.theatlantic.com/entertainment /archive/2011/06/100-acres-pizza-served-us-daily/351989.

"WHAT'S THE BIGGEST BURGER EVER MADE?" —MATT B.

Guinness World Records. "Largest Hamburger Patty," September 5, 1999, www.guinnessworldrecords.com/world-records/largest-hamburger -patty.

"WHAT'S THE FASTEST ANYONE CAN FLIP PANCAKES?" —LISA D.

Guinness World Records. "Most Tosses of a Pancake in One Minute," February 21, 2012, www.guinnessworldrecords.com/world-records /most-tosses-of-a-pancake-in-one-minute.

CHAPTER 4: YOUR LIFE IN NUMBERS

"HOW MANY TIMES DO WE BLINK WHILE WATCHING A MOVIE?" —ALEXIS V.

Stromberg, Joseph. "Why Do We Blink So Frequently?," *Smithsonian*, December 24, 2012, www.smithsonianmag.com/science-nature/why-do -we-blink-so-frequently-172334883/?no-ist.

"WHAT IS THE LONGEST JUMP ROPE SOMEONE USED TO JUMP ROPE?" —SAMANTHA D.

Guinness World Records. "Longest Rope Skipped," April 9, 2011, www .guinnessworldrecords.com/world-records/longest-rope-skipped.

Guinness World Records. "Most Dogs Skipping on the Same Rope," January 17, 2013, www.guinnessworldrecords.com/world-records /most-dogs-skipping-on-the-same-rope-.

Guinness World Records. "Most People Skipping on the Same Rope," January 11, 2016, www.guinnessworldrecords.com/world-records /most-people-skipping-on-the-same-rope.

"HOW MANY BALLOONS WOULD IT TAKE TO CARRY ME INTO THE AIR?" —DELILAH B.

Clark, Josh. "How Many Balloons Would It Take to Lift You off the Ground, Answered," *Stuff You Should Know*, June 18, 2013, www .stuffyoushouldknow.com/blog/balloons-lift-ground-answered.

"How many words can you say in a day?" —Simon G.

Liberman, Mark. "An Invented Statistic Returns," Language Log, February 22, 2013, languagelog.ldc.upenn.edu/nll/?p=4488.

"How fast do the balls travel in different sports, like tennis, soccer, baseball, lacrosse, and football?" —Callie S.

Breech, John. "Colin Kaepernick No Longer Has NFL Combine-Record for Fastest Pass," *CBS Sports*, March 3, 2014, www.cbssports.com/nfl/eye-on-football/24246665/colin-kaepernick-no-longer-has-nfl-combine-record-for-fastest-pass.

Hoch, Brian. "105.5! Hicks' throw fastest in Statcast era," April 21, 2016, m.mlb.com/news/article/173513490/yankees-aaron-hicks-throws-ball-1055-mph.

Infoplease. "Standard Measurements in Sports," www.infoplease.com/ipa/A0113430.html.

Guinness World Records. "Fastest Golf Drive," January 23, 2013, www.guinnessworldrecords.com/world-records/fastest-golf-drive.

Guinness World Records. "Fastest Lacrosse Shot," September 29, 2015, www.guinnessworldrecords.com/world-records/fastest-lacrosse-shot.

McLoughlin, Josh. "The 5 Fastest Shots Ever Recorded in Football," HITC Sport, www.hitc.com/en-gb/2013/10/24/jm-the-5-fastest-shots-ever-recorded-in-football.

National Football League Rulebook, static.nfl.com/static/content/public/image/rulebook/pdfs/5_2013_Ball.pdf.

Wikipedia, s.v. "Aroldis Chapman," last modified June 23, 2016, en.wikipedia.org/wiki/Aroldis_Chapman.

Wikipedia, s.v. "Fastest Recorded Tennis Serves," last modified June 24, 2016, en.wikipedia.org/wiki/Fastest_recorded_tennis_serves.

"How long ago did people start using last names?" —William O.

Blake, Paul. "What's In a Name? Your Link to the Past," Family History, BBC, April 26, 2011, www.bbc.co.uk/history/familyhistory/get_started/surnames_01.shtml.

Infoplease. "Most Common Last Names, 2010," www.infoplease.com/us/census/most-common-last-names-2010.html.

U.S. and World Population Clock, www.census.gov/popclock.

"How many cars can fit on a big highway at the same time?" —Albert W.

Liszka, Jason. "How Traffic Actually Works," October 1, 2013, jliszka.github.io/2013/10/01/how-traffic-actually-works.html.

Vanderbilt, Tom. *Traffic: Why We Drive the Way We Do*, New York: Vintage Books, 2008.

"How many times would the wheels of our car have to turn to travel all the way around the globe once?" —Thompson T.

Tire Size. "Tire Size Chart," tiresize.com/chart.

CHAPTER 5: EARTH AND FRIENDS

"What happens if you dig a hole straight down into the ground? How far until you reach the bottom?" —Ajax L.

Sharp, Tim. "How Big is Earth?," September 17, 2012, www.space.com/17638-how-big-is-earth.html.

"IF YOU TOOK THE PLASTIC BOTTLES USED IN 1 DAY AND WRAPPED THEM AROUND THE EARTH, HOW MANY TIMES WOULD THEY WRAP AROUND?" —CARTER F.

Ban the Bottle. "Bottled Water Facts," www.banthebottle.net/bottled-water-facts.

"HOW LONG WOULD IT TAKE TO RUN AROUND THE WORLD?" —VALERIA S.

McCoy, William. "Normal Speed for Jogging," Livestrong, April 25, 2015, www.livestrong.com/article/526358-normal-speed-for-jogging.

"HOW MANY SOCCER BALLS WOULD FIT INSIDE A HOLLOW EARTH?" —ALEX AND JACOB W.

FIFA Quality Program. "Circumference," quality.fifa.com/en/Footballs/Become-a-licensee/Tests/Circumference.

"HOW MANY LADDERS WOULD IT TAKE TO GET ME TO THE MOON?" —EVELYN L.

National Aeronautics and Space Administration. "How far away is the moon?," NASA Space Place, spaceplace.nasa.gov/moon-distance/en.

National Aeronautics and Space Administration. "Jupiter Fact Sheet," NASA Space Science Data Archive, nssdc.gsfc.nasa.gov/planetary/factsheet/jupiterfact.html.

National Aeronautics and Space Administration. "Mars Fact Sheet," NASA Space Science Data Archive, nssdc.gsfc.nasa.gov/planetary/factsheet/marsfact.html.

National Aeronautics and Space Administration. "Mercury Fact Sheet," NASA Space Science Data Archive, nssdc.gsfc.nasa.gov/planetary/factsheet/mercuryfact.html.

National Aeronautics and Space Administration. "Neptune Fact Sheet," NASA Space Science Data Archive, nssdc.gsfc.nasa.gov/planetary/factsheet/neptunefact.html.

National Aeronautics and Space Administration. "Planetary Fact Sheet: U.S. Units," NASA Space Science Data Archive, nssdc.gsfc.nasa.gov/planetary/factsheet/planet_table_british.html.

National Aeronautics and Space Administration. "Saturn Fact Sheet," NASA Space Science Data Archive, http://nssdc.gsfc.nasa.gov/planetary/factsheet/saturnfact.html.

National Aeronautics and Space Administration. "Uranus Fact Sheet," NASA Space Science Data Archive, http://nssdc.gsfc.nasa.gov/planetary/factsheet/uranusfact.html.

National Aeronautics and Space Administration. "Venus Fact Sheet," NASA Space Science Data Archive, http://nssdc.gsfc.nasa.gov/planetary/factsheet/venusfact.html.

"HOW MANY TIMES DOES EARTH GO AROUND THE SUN IN A YEAR?" —RUBY MAE C.

National Aeronautics and Space Administration. "Jupiter Fact Sheet," NASA Space Science Data Archive, nssdc.gsfc.nasa.gov/planetary/factsheet/jupiterfact.html.

National Aeronautics and Space Administration. "Mars Fact Sheet," NASA Space Science Data Archive, nssdc.gsfc.nasa.gov/planetary/factsheet/marsfact.html.

National Aeronautics and Space Administration. "Mercury Fact Sheet," NASA Space Science Data Archive, nssdc.gsfc.nasa.gov/planetary/factsheet/mercuryfact.html.

National Aeronautics and Space Administration. "Neptune Fact Sheet," NASA Space Science Data Archive, nssdc.gsfc.nasa.gov/planetary/factsheet/neptunefact.html.

"HOW BIG IS THE SUN? HOW MANY EARTHS COULD FIT INSIDE THE SUN?" —ELIJAH B.

National Aeronautics and Space Administration. "Sun: By the Numbers," solarsystem.nasa.gov/planets/sun/facts.

"ASSUMING YOU COULD SURVIVE THE HEAT, HOW LONG WOULD IT TAKE TO ORBIT THE SUN IN A SPACECRAFT?" —SEBASTIAN B.

Riebeek, Holly. "Catalog of Earth Satellite Orbits," National Aeronautics and Space Administration, Earth Observatory, September 4, 2009, earthobservatory.nasa.gov/Features/OrbitsCatalog.

"Kepler's Three Laws." The Physics Classroom, 2016, http://www.physicsclassroom.com/class/circles/Lesson-4/Kepler-s-Three-Law.

"HOW LONG WOULD IT TAKE TO TRAVEL TO PLUTO?" —VICTORIA AND EMILIA I.

Talbert, Tricia, ed. "New Horizons: The First Mission to the Pluto System and the Kuiper Belt," National Aeronautics and Space Administration, August 24, 2105, www.nasa.gov/mission_pages/newhorizons/overview/index.html.

Davis, Phillips, ed. "Pluto: Overview: King of the Kuiper Belt," National Aeronautics and Space Administration, solarsystem.nasa.gov/planets/pluto.

THANK YOU FOR READING THIS
FEIWEL AND FRIENDS BOOK.

···················· The Friends who made ····················

How Many
GUINEA PIGS
Can Fit
ON A PLANE?

ANSWERS TO YOUR MOST
CLEVER MATH QUESTIONS

···················· possible are: ····················

JEAN FEIWEL, *Publisher*

LIZ SZABLA, *Associate Publisher*

RICH DEAS, *Senior Creative Director*

HOLLY WEST, *Editor*

ALEXEI ESIKOFF, *Senior Managing Editor*

KIM WAYMER, *Senior Production Manager*

ANNA ROBERTO, *Editor*

CHRISTINE BARCELLONA, *Associate Editor*

KAT BRZOZOWSKI, *Editor*

ANNA POON, *Assistant Editor*

EMILY SETTLE, *Administrative Assistant*

PATRICK COLLINS, *Creative Director*

ILANA WORRELL, *Production Editor*

Follow us on Facebook or visit
us online at mackids.com

OUR BOOKS ARE FRIENDS FOR LIFE